THEY WANT ME TO BE AN ELDER!

WHAT DO THEY DO?

THEY WANT ME TO BE AN ELDER!

WHAT DO THEY DO?

Brian Winslade

Oikos Books
Private Bag 3120, Waikato Mail Centre, Hamilton 3240, NZ

ISBN 978-0-473-43668-1

Formerly published as: Elders . . . and their place in our church (1994)

Cover Design by Luke Winslade
(luke.winslade@gmail.com)

Published by Oikos Books

Printed by Your Books
16 Cashew St, Grenada North, Wellington 5028, NZ

By the same author:

Shifting the Paradigms of The Normal Christian Church (1994)

Baptism in Water & The Spirit (Oikos Books, 1995, 2008)

Lord of All (Oikos Books, 2002)

A New Kind of Baptist Church – Reframing Congregational Government for the 21st Century (Morling Press, 2010)

CONTENTS

PREFACE

My experience with a governance team of elders has been exceedingly positive. In the churches that I have pastored over the last forty years I consider myself greatly blessed by teams of elders who have nurtured me through seasons of growth and helped mold my thinking about leadership in the church. I have enjoyed the challenge of making myself accountable to an eldership over aspects of my ministry and leadership. At times they have disagreed with my judgment, and even brought gentle rebuke over actions I have taken, or words spoken. That is never easy to receive, but I am grateful to God for a team of leaders who have cared enough for me to speak the truth in love.

Pastoral ministry is at times a lonely calling. In terms of philosophy of ministry, I am totally committed to the team approach. The church is too important to be left in the leadership hands of one person, and I don't trust my own judgment sufficiently to be left to my own devices. I regard myself as a part of the eldership of the churches I have pastored, not separate from it or over it. Mutual accountability is probably the best way to describe our relationship. Together we exercise our leadership function. To use a sporting analogy, some of us play better in different positions on the field, and each team requires a captain, but the strength of the team comes from all the players, not just one.

While my experience with governing elders has been exceedingly positive, the experience of others has sometimes been the opposite. Many people have been hurt and confused over ill-defined roles and expectations of those called to the office of elder. What elders are expected to do in the life of the church has been a source of hot debate for some. In helping a particular church through this kind of confusion I looked around for good material that I could put into the hands of people: some sound biblical exposition on the office and expectations of those called to eldership. Perhaps I failed to look in the right places, but I couldn't find a great deal. That concerned me, as the appointment of people to the office of elder is probably one of the more crucial appointments in the life of a local church.

Having failed to find someone who had done my homework for me, I decided to make the matter of eldership a subject of my own study. Like many churches, the one where this project had its genesis had had its fair share of conflict and tumult with respect to leadership definition. The human source of this in many cases had been, in my opinion, a weak grasp of what the Bible actually teaches about the office of elder. That which follows began as a series of messages on the subject of eldership in the lead up to an appointment process. Several pastor-colleagues began asking for copies of my sermon notes, which is how this little book came into being. In one small way, this is my effort to address and set forth for the future a foundation for church leadership that is consistent with Scripture.

A word of explanation is called for in respect to gender. It might appear from what follows that I perceive of the office of elder as being the domain of men only, as the masculine pronoun is what is almost always used. This is simply so for grammatical expediency. While not everyone has the capacity or calling for leadership, I am convinced that leadership offices in the church are gender neutral. To be sure, the Apostle Paul spoke of elders in his writings with the masculine pronoun, but there are several cultural and historical factors that need to be remembered. Likewise, Paul acknowledged many women in leadership and apostolic-type roles in the churches of his day, and I personally believe he would do so today in respect to eldership. From Pentecost onwards the issue is character and gifting, not gender.

When first published (1994) this work contained just three chapters. Over the years I have observed a number of local church conflicts emerge from misunderstood processes when church members present to elders complaints or accusations of misconduct. Unless handled wisely, these can have a disastrous effect upon the unity and function of a leadership team. A fourth Chapter has been added with respect to elders ill-advisedly attempting to play the role of ombudsmen within a local church.

I also acknowledge that not every church in our day and age appoints people to a leadership office entitled "elder." While that is clearly the terminology Paul employed in the New Testament era, many other names are used for leadership positions in the contemporary church (e.g. board, diaconate, overseers, vestry, council, etc.), and I do not believe this is in conflict with the biblical model. While this publication uses the term "elder," the principles are easily transferable to other titled leadership positions in the church.

What follows is not presented as a rigorous academic work, although hopefully able to withstand such scrutiny. Nor does it project as the final word on this subject. Think of it more like a fireside chat, deliberately written in *first person* narrative, to those contemplating what it means to serve as an elder in God's church.

Brian Winslade
New Zealand, 2018

ONE
THE OFFICE & FUNCTION OF AN ELDER

Virtually all of my Christian experience has been within the "free church" stream. Almost all the churches within this ecclesiastical stream are today made up of people from a wide variety of traditions and Christian experience. They may have participated in several other churches prior to becoming a part of the one they now call home, and in many cases have tasted several different denominational styles. Inevitably some of the background, perspective and ecclesiology from past experience is brought into the current situation. The typical contemporary or cosmopolitan congregation can be like a two-edged sword. On the one hand there is a great deal of creativity and freshness when people of different backgrounds are brought together. On the other hand, there can also occur serious clashes of conviction and opinion. We differ, sometimes strongly, on certain peripheral matters of doctrine or office in the church.

In those churches with which I have been involved a wide variety of views and opinions have surfaced about what eldership looks like, and the nature of their responsibilities. Some of these convictions have been so entrenched as to threaten the unity and harmony of the church as a whole. In fact, on more than one occasion I have seen people leave their church and join another over conflicting opinion about the role and performance of elders.

While my calling to pastoral ministry has been within the Baptist stream of churches, that which I set forth here is not peculiarly a "Baptist position" of eldership, but (hopefully) a biblical one. In fact, there is no such thing as a "Baptist position" on eldership. The emergence of the office of elders in Baptist churches is only relatively recent - a matter of a few decades.[1] There is very little tradition and history over the last 400 years on which to draw except, of course, for the Scriptures. In terms of a denominational position, if it is reflected and taught in the Bible then that is a Baptist position; if it is not clearly grounded in the Scriptures then we don't want a bar of it.

In order to gain a broad biblical perspective on the role and function of eldership we will consider a variety of passages that make mention of the term. These will help us piece together a profile of what an elder is and does.

Before doing that, however, let me state my conviction that biblical teaching on matters of church government and organisation is largely pragmatic, rather than prescriptive. By pragmatic I mean, if it works, use it! There is not one specific description of how churches should be structured, and what those in positions of leadership should do or be called. What we do find in the Scriptures are principles of leadership. Some people have formed

---

[1] The historical tradition in Baptist churches has tended to regard the pastor as an/the elder; supported by a diaconate or court of deacons as the collective governance body to whom functional leadership has been delegated from the church Members' Meeting, although this has changed dramatically over the last few decades as more and more churches appoint elders

very strong views on how a church should be organised and governed and argue that their perspective is that found in the New Testament. Others dispute that and insist that their perspective or style of church government is what the Bible teaches.

Arguments along these lines, in my opinion, are largely a waste of time. When we have a particular perspective well established in our minds it is not too difficult to make the Bible say what we want it to say, based on favourite and selective proof-texts. I don't believe that all of the New Testament churches were structured and organised in exactly the same way. Each operated in divergent circumstances and contexts, and had a different corporate personality from other churches. What the New Testament does speak more clearly of is principles of leadership. Most of those principles have to do with the character and qualifications of leaders, rather than their specific job descriptions.

Church Government

There are three main philosophies of church government and authority that have manifested over the past twenty centuries. In each of them the Spirit of God has seen fit to move and bless. And also, in each of them, he has found his work constricted and quenched.

The oldest form or style of church government is that known as *episkopalianism*, where the church is governed by bishops (*episkopos*) and priests. While Christ is always acknowledged as the head of the church, temporal authority rests (or is vested) in one person or a hierarchy or a chain of command. Power to rule or direct the church is in the hands of the leader of the church. The rank-and-file might influence or advise, but the ultimate authority, under God, rests with the leader. This kind of church government would describe churches like the Roman Catholic or Anglican or Lutheran church, but not exclusively. It would also describe the church government style of some Pentecostal churches where the pastor is perceived as the functional authority (under God) and calls the tune, or likewise hierarchical movements like the Salvation Army.

The second form of church government is that known as *presbyterianism*, and has emerged over the last 400 years. In this concept of church leadership, the authority or power does not rest in the hands of just one person (the leader), but in a group of leaders. An eldership or collegiate of leaders direct the affairs of the church. This kind of church government describes churches like the Presbyterians, Methodists and Reformed churches, and also churches like the Open Brethren. Authority rests, not with one man, but with a group of leaders.

The third concept of church government is known as *congregationalism*, where the ultimate temporal authority in the church rests with the congregation or membership as a whole. Each congregation is autonomous from a denominational hierarchy, and appoints its own leadership, but those in leadership are still subject to the final authority of the membership as a whole. The church members' meeting can both appoint and dismiss those in leadership, and if necessary override their decisions. This kind of church government describes churches such as Congregationalist and Baptist, among others.

Virtually every type of church can be characterised by one of these three types of church government or authority. And as I say, through each of them the Spirit of God has found liberty to move and bless, and in each he has been constricted and grieved. Each might claim that theirs is closest to what the Bible teaches, but

God seems to work through or in spite of them all.

Personally, I feel uncomfortable with power and authority in the church resting in the hands of just one person. As a pastor, while I am a fairly incisive person with strong leadership gifting, I greatly appreciate the creative tension of having to work with and convince a group of fellow elders of a course of action that I think we should take. On several occasions their collective wisdom has kept me from making unwise leadership decisions. Lord Acton's famous phrase: "Power tends to corrupt, and absolute power corrupts absolutely" has proven all to true in many churches where leaders have wielded too much power. Having a wider counsel of people to test and verify the direction in which a leader believes the Lord is leading, is a tremendous safeguard. Likewise, those in leadership need to be accountable to the wider family of the church. Leadership in any form that is not accountable, or dismissible, can sometimes be only one step away from the single authoritarian leader.

On the other side of the ledger, although I have grown up within the Baptist denomination, I don't always feel comfortable with some of the classical congregational model of church government either. In its extreme, every church decision is perceived to be subject to the democratic vote of its members. This is a chronic recipe for inertia. Congregationalism does not imply the leadership of *none*, nor the leadership or management of *all*. God has always raised up people to be leaders in his church, and leaders need to be allowed to lead, not constantly held back by the consensus and democracy of a church meeting. Indeed, the Bible teaches both the principles of leadership and followership, and both are necessary in a healthy church.

I guess the ultimate style of church government to aim

for is that known as a *theocracy*, where the ultimate leader and authority in our church is Jesus. Government is not by autocracy (the pastor) or oligarchy (the elders), nor by democracy (the congregational vote), but by theocracy, where God (*theo*) is the leader of the church. He is the King, and like Israel 3000 years ago, we don't need a man (or group of men) to rule over us. God is in charge, and God can speak and direct through any and all of us. We are able to hear his voice and direction through whomever it might come, from the newest Christian to the oldest. That is some of what we understand by the (New Testament) doctrine of the "priesthood of all believers". No intermediaries are necessary. All of us can hear and speak the word of God; we are all priests.

Now, it is possible to take that to an illogical extreme, and some have tended to do so. They claim that because Jesus is the head of his church it is therefore not necessary to have appointed leaders in the local church at all. "If we are all priests unto God, might offices of church leadership, organisation and systems be totally unnecessary, and hinder what God wants to do?" This kind of thinking, coupled with many serious instances of abuse by leaders, has fed a growing dissatisfaction and disillusionment with the whole notion of organised church and leadership structures. Growing numbers of Christians have simply opted out of church life altogether.

There is a lot that could be said on this issue. Suffice it to say that it is, in my opinion, a serious denial of the biblical pattern. The model in Scripture is quite clear. Whenever God had dealings with his people, he raised up a man or a woman who would lead them. God was always in charge and the ultimate leader of the people of Israel, but it was also God's choice to raise up people like Moses and Joshua, Gideon, Deborah and David,

Paul and John and Barnabas (to name a few) who were appointed leaders under God for specific times and seasons. The principle of systemic leadership amongst the people of God is quite clear and unmistakably demonstrated within the Scriptures.

New Testament Model

When it came to planting churches, Paul and Barnabas obviously had a similar understanding in each of the churches they established. Luke makes special record of it in Acts 14:23:

> *Paul and Barnabas appointed elders for them in each church and, with prayer and fasting, committed them to the Lord, in whom they had put their trust.*

Whenever new churches were established, leadership was appointed to help in the directing and growth of the church. Elders were not the exclusive recipients of the word of the Lord for a local church - Paul's teaching on spiritual gifts makes that abundantly clear - but it was also God's pattern to appoint people to offices of leadership and oversight.

What exactly did these elders in the New Testament churches do? What was their function and responsibility? To see how the New Testament church understood the office of eldership we need to go back to the original language in which the New Testament was written. There are two key Greek words used by writers of the New Testament (and they appear to be used interchangeably) both referring to the same office.

The first is the word *episkopos* which has traditionally been translated in to English as "bishop". A better and more literal rendition, which we find in some of the newer translations, is that of "overseer". *Episkopos* is derived from two words - *epi*, meaning over, and *skopeo*, meaning to look or watch.

In the culture of the day in which the New Testament was written, *episkopos* or overseer described a person (or group of people) who kept watch over a country or region or a local community and exercised a supervisory and a management function. They ensured that the affairs of the state or the community were carried out. They were responsible for governance, and for seeing that the aims and objectives of the community were adhered to. They ensured that disputes between conflicting parties were being settled. Standing a step back from "hands-on" involvement in the affairs of the community to be able to get the bigger picture, they watched over the community as a whole and made sure that everything was running according to schedule. Within the concept of *episkopos* was an authority to lead and direct the affairs of the community so that everyone was benefited.

The second word is *presbyteros*, which is almost always translated in to English as "elder". It stems from a word used to refer to people of older age, but the concept of *presbyteros* was not necessarily limited to someone who was older chronologically. Timothy, for instance, was presumed to be an elder in the church, but we know from Paul's instruction to him that he was relatively young. The meaning of *presbyteros* had to do with perceived maturity and wisdom, with someone looked up to as able to give wise counsel or advice, someone whose judgement was respected. Revered as leaders because of their proven wisdom and maturity, elders were regarded as like spiritual fathers (and mothers) in the family of the church.

Both of these words are used interchangeably in the New Testament, and Biblical scholars seem to all agree that they refer to the same position.[2] The idea of the *overseer* describes the function that they perform in terms of governance and authority, and the title of *elder* describes their spiritual maturity and the respect with which they are held. They give us a good picture of the nature and importance of elders and help us see why Paul and Barnabas appointed them in each of the churches they planted.

But how are these functions to be carried out? What are some of the specific responsibilities of those we call elders?

In answering that question it would be very helpful if we could open the Scriptures to a succinct passage that outlines their job description in detail. "The role of an elder is to . . ." Unfortunately, in the wisdom of God we don't have that kind of passage to turn to. Instead, what we do have are numerous passages or texts that refer to the office of eldership, perhaps like little pieces of a jigsaw. When we take each piece and put it together with all the other little pieces, we can begin to see a pattern emerging.

Let's take a look at a variety of scriptures, starting in the Old Testament and working through to the New, noting examples of eldership function that we find. This of course is not an exhaustive list, but if we're going to hold a strong opinion on the office of eldership, let's at least make sure that it is based on what the Bible says.

To start with we look at Moses and an emerging leadership amongst the community of Israel. In Numbers 11:16,17 we read these words:

> *The Lord said to Moses: `Bring me seventy of Israel's elders who are known to you as leaders and officials among the*

---

[2] When Paul called for a meeting with the elders of the Ephesian church (Acts 20) he summons *presbyters* (20:17), and when they meet together he refers to them as *bishops* (20:28).

people. Have them come to the Tent of Meeting, that they may stand there with you. I will come down and speak with you there, and I will take of the Spirit that is on you and put the Spirit on them. They will help you carry the burden of the people so that you will not have to carry it alone.'

The burden of responsibility for leadership in the community of Israel was to be shared by the elders, not carried by Moses alone. The elders were to assist Moses in his pastoral and leadership function. To put that another way, the burden of leadership responsibility was not to be carried by just one person, but by a group of leaders. Moses was not the only one to whom the people could turn when a problem arose. They could also turn to those in eldership.

Going back a book to Leviticus 4 we read an example of an interesting role for elders in acting out the corporate repentance of the people of God when they sin. v.13-15:

If the whole Israelite community sins unintentionally and does what is forbidden in any of the Lord's commands, even though the community is unaware of the matter, they are guilty. When they become aware of the sin they committed, the assembly must bring a young bull as a sin offering and present it before the Tent of Meeting. The elders of the community are to lay their hands on the bull's head before the Lord, and the bull shall be slaughtered before the Lord . . .

Now, there is no doubt a great deal more to understand here about the significance of what the elders were asked to do, but it is an interesting illustration of a function of elders in the ministry of intercession. The elders were to intercede for (in the literal interpretation of the word - "stand in the place of") the people. Before God, they symbolised the corporate repentance of God's people, and sought his forgiveness. Bringing that as a principle into the Christian church, an important function of eldership involves praying for God's mercy and forgiveness and cleansing for the church, interceding on behalf of the church, pleading the cause of the people before the throne of God. Or as I heard it expressed once: Not merely spending time with the people about the things of God; also spending time with God about the things of the people!

Moving forward to the book of Ruth, we read in the fourth chapter of a function of eldership as the dispensing or ensuring of justice. Boaz wanted to make a just transaction with one of his relatives, and in order to be sure he was doing things right, he asked some of the elders of his community to witness it. Verse four reads:

> *I thought I should bring the matter to your attention and suggest that you buy it in the presence of these seated here and in the presence of the elders of my people . . .*

In other words, the elders in Israel acted in a judicial function, attesting that matters were handled fairly and adjudicating in matters of dispute between two parties. That is a legitimate function of those in eldership. They lend wisdom and counsel in matters of conflict and settle disputes that need an intermediary or an adjudicator.

Proverbs 31 gives a beautiful description of a godly woman, with examples of her character. In v.23 there is a little snippet of information, that is not central to the point of the text, but does illustrate something about the function of elders in the nation of Israel:

> *Her husband is respected at the city gate, where he takes his seat among the elders of the land . . .*

Where would you find the elders of the city? Seated around the gate of the city. In the world of Bible times, those responsible for the governance of a community watched and oversaw the comings and the goings of people. They noted who came in and what they brought with them, and they noted those who were leaving.

Now, there may well be other ways of interpreting this, but in many contemporary churches the responsibility for how people enter the formal membership of a local church family has been delegated to the elders.[3] In the figurative sense, they sit at the church gate and watch those coming in, and those going out, "overseeing our comings and goings".

Moving forward into the New Testament, there are a number of references to the office of eldership. In Acts 15 it was the elders in the church in Jerusalem who prayed and deliberated over the settling of a very serious theological dispute that had arisen concerning the expression of Christian faith amongst diverse ethnicities . They exercised a spiritual judicial function, determining the direction in which God was leading the church.

In Acts 20:17 Paul wrote to the church at Ephesus and invited himself along to one of their elders' meetings. Among other

---

[3] In my early years as a Baptist pastor church membership was granted by resolution of a church Members' Meeting. But this became impractical a) as churches became large and knowledge of candidates was less known, or b) if there were reasons for refusing membership this was essentially a pastoral matter that might require confidentiality and discretion – rather than splayed in front of the whole church membership!

things he had to say to them, he gave them these instructions about their function and responsibilities. v.28-31:

> *Keep watch over yourselves and all the flock of which the Holy Spirit has made you overseers. Be shepherds of the church of God, which he bought with his own blood. I know that after I leave, savage wolves will come in among you and will not spare the flock. Even from your own number men will arise and distort the truth in order to draw away disciples after them . . .*

In terms of definitions of words used, there are at least three functions that Paul mentions for elders in the church to fulfil. The first is what I refer to as governance. They were to oversee the affairs of the church, in terms of the meaning of *episkopos*. Seeing that the church fulfilled all its function. Secondly, they were to protect the flock from false teaching. It is the function of elders to counter or refute that which is taught or done in the life of a church when it conflicts with the God's counsel. If we are living in the latter days before the return of Christ such a function will become more and more evident. Thirdly, Paul talks about elders as shepherds of the flock. In the days in which the Scriptures were written, there were two main functions that a shepherd had. One was to provide food and nurture for the flock. The second was to protect them from impending danger. The shepherd guarded or protected the sheep from the wolf or lion that might attack them.

The English words "shepherd" and "pastor" are both translated from the same Greek word *poimen*. To be a shepherd is to exercise a pastoral function. In that sense elders are to be like shepherds to the family of God, making sure that the church is spiritually nourished and encouraged, and protected from false doctrine.

In that regard, however, some have tended to see the function of eldership in a way that I think is too narrow. Eldership does not exactly equate with the function of pastoring. Shepherding or pastoral care is one of the functions of elders, but not the sum total of their responsibilities. Their task is to ensure that shepherding takes place. However, there may be many others in the family of God who also have pastoral or shepherding gifts which need to be employed.

In the first of Peter's letters there is a similar exhortation to that which Paul gave to the Ephesians.

> *1 Peter 5:1-3*
> *To the elders among you, I appeal as a fellow elder, a witness of Christ's suffering and one who also will share in the glory to be revealed: Be shepherds of God's flock that is under your care, serving as overseers - not because you must, but because you are willing, as God wants you to be; not greedy for money, but eager to serve; not lording it over those entrusted to you, but being examples to the flock . . .*

The role of an elder is to model what it means to follow Jesus, not telling others to "do as I say!" but rather "do as I do". How did Paul put it in 1 Corinthians 11:1? *"Follow my example as I follow the example of Christ."* The call to eldership is the call to role modelling.

When the Apostle Paul wrote his first letter to Timothy he was obviously very much concerned about the matter of eldership in that church. He gave very detailed instructions about the qualifications for those who are appointed as elders, and in the next chapter we will examine these more closely. But he also gave two other little snippets of information about the function of an elder.

1 Timothy 4:14
Do not neglect your gift, which was given you through a prophetic message when the body of elders laid their hands on you . . .

1 Timothy 5:17
The elders who direct the affairs of the church well are worthy of double honour, especially those whose work is preaching and teaching . . .

Once again there is a great deal that could be expounded from these two verses, but in brief they indicate that the elders in the New Testament church obviously laid hands on people and prayed for them. They prophesied over people and were used by God in the impartation of spiritual gifts and power ministry. Secondly, the elders were also involved in the ministry of the word. They were people who taught the Scriptures, and who built up others with the counsel of God's word.

There is no doubt many other references to eldership functions in the New Testament, but the last I want to cite is from James, the brother of Jesus. In James 5:14-15 we read:

Is any one of you sick? He should call the elders of the church to pray over him and anoint him with oil in the name of the Lord. And the prayer offered in faith will make the sick person well; the Lord will raise him up . . .

This is not to imply that elders are the only ones in the church who should lay hands on the sick and pray for healing. Neither does it infer that having the spiritual "gift" of healing is one of the prerequisite qualifications for being an elder. (I've heard that suggested, and I think it is nonsense!) Many within the body of Christ will have gifting and faith to pray for the sick, and some of them may in fact be among those appointed as elders. What James was referring to here, I believe, was a special function or spiritual authority that the body of elders in a church have in respect to praying for healing. It is one of their responsibilities to be available to go and pray for the sick. The elders are not the only ones who can do so, but it is definitely a part of their function.

As stated, the Scriptures listed above are far from an exhaustive list of references to eldership in the Old and New Testament. To summarise, however, we have noted at least eleven specific functions of those appointed to the office of elder amongst God's community:

1. Sharing the load of leadership
2. Intercession
3. Ensuring/dispensing justice
4. Overseeing the gateway into the church
5. Discerning the will of God
6. Governance and oversight
7. Refuting false teaching
8. Shepherding and pastoral care
9. Laying hands on people (prophesying)
10. Preaching and teaching
11. Praying for the sick

Next, we need to consider some of the qualifications necessary for a person to be appointed to the office of elder.

TWO
QUALIFICATIONS FOR ELDERSHIP

Having outlined some of the responsibilities of, and the mandate for elders, we now turn our attention to how people are selected for such an office. How do we recognise a potential elder? What kinds of qualifications are we to look for? As it is a position of considerable influence in the life of a church, much care is called for in the selection and appointment of the right people to the office.

Perhaps one way of determining who should or shouldn't be appointed to the office of elder is to look at those functions listed in Chapter One and see who most adequately fulfils them. Are those nominated for eldership competent or able to fulfil the responsibilities of that office? However, as we will note in a moment, function is only one part of the eldership equation. There are also many aspects of character that need to be considered.

The question of who should and who shouldn't be appointed to eldership was an issue that some of the New Testament churches obviously wrestled with. The Apostle Paul wrote to at least two pastors, and their respective churches, giving detailed instruction on qualifications to look for. The letters he wrote to Timothy and Titus contain the clearest criteria we find in Scripture for the selection of elders.

> *1 Timothy 3:1-7*
> *Here is a trustworthy saying: If anyone sets his heart on being an overseer, he desires a noble task. Now the overseer must be above reproach, the husband of but one wife, temperate, self-controlled, respectable, hospitable, able to teach, not given to drunkenness, not violent but gentle, not quarrelsome, not a lover of money. He must manage his own family well and see that his children obey him with proper respect. (If anyone does not know how to manage his own family, how can he take care of God's church?) He must not be a recent convert, or he may become conceited and fall under the same judgment as the devil. He must also have a good reputation with outsiders, so that he will not fall into disgrace and into the devil's trap.*

> *Titus 1:5-9*
> *The reason I left you in Crete was that you might straighten out what was left unfinished and appoint elders in every town, as I directed you. An elder must be blameless, the husband of but one wife, a man whose children believe and are not open to the charge of being wild and disobedient. Since an overseer is entrusted with God's work, he must be blameless - not overbearing, not quick-tempered, not given to drunkenness, not violent, not pursuing dishonest gain. Rather he must be hospitable, one who loves what is good, who is self-controlled, upright, holy and disciplined. He must hold firmly to the trustworthy message as it has been taught,*

so that he can encourage others by sound doctrine and refute those who oppose it.

Character, rather than gifting

Before examining each of the qualities that Paul mentions in these passages, there are one or two comments by way of overview that need to be made. The first is that, according to the teaching of Paul, qualifications for the office of elder are a matter of character, rather than gifting. When Paul wrote to Timothy and Titus about who should be appointed as elders in the church he does not list certain "gifts" of the Spirit that must be evident or manifested in the person under consideration. Rather, he lists character traits. The notable absence of spiritual gifting in Paul's list of qualifications is rather interesting. Instead, what he majors on are attributes of character and spiritual maturity.

In that light, we need to view the appointment of people to the office of elder in a somewhat different manner from the way we recognise people with an office or function that is related to a specific "gifting." What do I mean by that? The office of elder in the local church is not necessarily related to a particular "gift mix." For instance, recognising and appointing an elder is not the same as, say, recognising and "setting apart" an evangelist. We recognise the calling on a person to be an evangelist because of the way the Lord uses them in bringing people into relationship with Jesus. Likewise, with the person who is recognised as a prophet or a pastor, or maybe a missionary who serves abroad. Their gifting is recognised and appreciated by others, and on the basis of their observed competence in that field, they are seen as having a special role or ministry in the life of the church.

When it comes to the office of elder there is a different set of criteria. When Paul listed the qualities to look for he didn't spell out a list of spiritual gifts.[4] Rather, the qualities to look for are matters of character and maturity and godliness.

It's perhaps not central to the teaching of these texts, but an interesting implication of what Paul wrote to Timothy and Titus is that elders are in fact to be selected and appointed. Entering in to the office of elder is not something that happens automatically or mysteriously. Nor is it to be viewed as a kind of merit badge or honorific title for those who have served well in the church over many years. The context in which Paul wrote indicated a very definite selection of people, not something that happened secretly or shrouded in mystical prophetic revelation. Paul was giving Timothy and Titus, and their respective churches, a check-list by which they could assess or eliminate those who might be considered for the office of elder.

There are many ways churches make their selection of elders. In some churches the Pastor selects and appoints those in eldership. That way he or she can be sure they have a team that they can work productively with. On the negative side, it would be easy to select only those people a pastor knows will support them in whatever they suggest. In other churches the existing eldership makes the selection and appointment of those who should join their number: a kind of self-perpetuating body. In some churches, selection of elders has been left to the visiting prophet or apostle who comes in and spends time with the church. In the stream of churches that I have served within, appointment to eldership is something for which the whole church family has a say. While those in leadership consider and formally nominate those people

4 Two possible exceptions to that might be "hospitality" and "teaching," which Paul in other places cites as gifts of the Spirit, but whether he was thinking here in terms of spiritual gifts is debatable.

who have been suggested to them, it is the consensus of the whole church body that actually makes the final decision. Not everyone who is nominated gets in, but those who do know they have the support and recognition of a very large majority of the church family.

Without wanting to debate the methodology of appointment of people to eldership, I contend it is important that there be some opportunity for review of performance. In the churches I have pastored, for instance, appointment of all lay leadership positions is for a defined term, after which re-appointment is necessary. In some churches, once you are appointed to eldership you are pretty well there for life, regardless of your performance. It is a very healthy practice in the life of a church where those in leadership, from time to time, allow the body to reaffirm their confidence in them. If members don't have confidence in them, they must be able to express it in some way. Without opportunity for review we sometimes give people little option but to vote with their feet, and that has become an unhealthy trend in the contemporary church.

Qualities for us all - not just elders

The point also needs to be made that the qualities that Paul lists for those in eldership are actually no different from those which we should all be aspiring to in our walk with the Lord. The kind of spiritual maturity expected of those in eldership is exactly the same as that which God asks from each of us. The point of separation is that those in leadership are to be good models of spiritual maturity. When Peter wrote to elders in 1 Peter 5:3 he encouraged them to *"be examples to the flock."* Likewise, Paul told the Corinthians to *"follow my example as I follow the example of Christ."* Leadership in the Kingdom of God is always out front and by example, never shouting orders from the back or the sideline. Elders are to lead their flock into spiritual maturity, modelling the role themselves.

Now let us turn our attention to the specifics of what Paul laid down to Timothy and Titus as prerequisite qualities in an elder. There are twenty attributes or characteristics mentioned in these two passages, the majority of them are mentioned in both. An elder must be:

1. Above reproach
2. Husband of one wife
3. Temperate
4. Self-controlled
5. Respectable
6. Hospitable
7. Able to teach
8. Not given to wine
9. Not overbearing
10. Not quick tempered
11. Not violent
12. Not quarrelsome
13. Gentle
14. Not a lover of money
15. Able to manage own household
16. Of good reputation
17. Lover of what is good
18. Upright outside church
19. Holy & disciplined
20. Not a new convert

There is enough material here to write a whole chapter on each, and numerous books have in fact been written on that basis. In order to give a brief summary, however, these twenty character-qualities might be grouped under the following four broad headings, each dealing with an important facet of personal life:

1. Reputation
2. Spiritual Maturity
3. Interpersonal Relationship Skills
4. Family Life

Specks and Planks!

Before looking at them in more detail, an appeal needs to be made for grace on behalf of those who might be asked to assume the role of elders. When we look closely at what Paul wrote about the character of an elder, I don't know too many who might ever qualify. But I don't think that was Paul's intent. When Paul gave a list of qualities by which we can attest or eliminate would-be elders, he is not giving us license to judge our brothers and sisters in Christ. These qualities are not a score card. And we need to bring alongside what Paul said the teaching of Jesus about specks and planks in each other's eyes. Be careful that the speck of dust we see in the eye of others is not a reflection of the plank of wood in our own! Our recognition of the faults and shortcomings in others may well be symptomatic of the fact that we too are sinners in the same area. If we have a weakness or propensity to sin in a certain area, it's not difficult to see the weaknesses of others in a similar light. Judge not, Jesus said, so that we will not be judged.

1. The Reputation of an Elder

Paul uses four words or phrases to describe the way in which a person qualified for eldership is regarded by others: Above *reproach, respectable, upright, and having a good reputation with outsiders.*

In other words, the man or woman of God is recognisable. He or she stands out in the crowd as a person of integrity and honesty. The word respectable means simply the person who is able to be respected. Someone whom it is possible to look up to and trust, whose judgment and counsel you know to be reliable. The original Greek word translated there as respectable is the word *kosmios*, which means literally "orderly." Their life is in order, rather than in chaos.

To be above reproach obviously doesn't mean to be perfect. None of us would qualify if that were the case. Rather, it speaks of people who don't have a cloud of doubt hanging over their heads as to their honesty. They are people of integrity. They mean what they say, and they say what they mean. When something delicate or confidential is entrusted to them, you know it can be trusted. They are well thought of, honoured and looked up to. Other people speak well of them.

In Acts 16:2 we read of how Paul first heard about Timothy:

> *. . . all the believers in Lystra and Iconium spoke well of Timothy.*

We can recognise the qualities of a godly person by how others speak of them. One person might be a close friend and speak in complimentary terms, but when more than one person speaks the same way, the reputation is a little more substantiated. In Timothy's case there was even a third testimony to his character:

people from more than one location (Lystra and Iconium) spoke positively about him. There is the test of a good reputation.

It is also interesting that Paul lists as a qualification for eldership the reputation a person holds with those outside the family of God. It might be possible to put on a religious mask when in the company of fellow believers, but what do those in the market place think? How do their non-Christian neighbours regard them? What about those they work with or their employees? Do they have a reputation in the town for honesty and fairness? How do they treat people - fairly and gently, or harshly?

Obviously, we need to consider the fact that being a Christian is going to bring us into conflict with the ways of the world. Sometimes we will be criticised and maligned for our righteousness. Some people will speak badly of the most saintly person, simply because they have a relationship with Jesus. But it's worth listening to how the unbeliever views our character and integrity. Our brothers and sisters in Christ are probably easier to fool than are those who don't know the Lord. Maybe that's why Paul wrote this way in Colossians 4:5-6:

> *Be wise in the way you act toward outsiders; make the most of every opportunity. Let your conversation be always full of grace, seasoned with salt, so that you may know how to answer everyone.*

Likewise, 1 Peter 2:12:

> *Live such good lives among the pagans that, though they accuse you of doing wrong, they may see your good deeds and glorify God on the day he visits us.*

The godly person who is qualified for the office of elder is well regarded, across the board, by many people and in many situations, even by those outside the church. He has a good and a commendable reputation.

2. The Spiritual Maturity of an Elder

There are six words or phrases that Paul uses to describe the kind of spiritual maturity an elder must display: *Not a new convert, self-controlled, not given to wine, not a lover of money, someone who loves what is good, holy and disciplined.*

Why would Paul suggest that an elder shouldn't be a new convert? In 1 Timothy 3:6 he gives the answer:

> *. . . he may become conceited and fall under the same judgment as the devil.*

Remember what happened to the devil? Once the highest-ranking angel in heaven, he became conceited and proud. He looked at the honour that God received and began to think of himself as worthy of similar homage. His pride in position was his downfall.

Many a new Christian has fallen into the same trap. Pushed into prominence and public profile too soon, before having the wisdom and experience that only time can bring, he becomes easy prey for the enemy. Full of energy and enthusiasm for the Lord, he looks in judgment and cynicism at those longer-in-the-spiritual-tooth, criticising them for not being as enthusiastic as he is. Youthful enthusiasm and idealism needs to be tempered with experience and realism.

Spiritual maturity is not something we can acquire overnight.

We can't get it from a Bible study course. It takes years. It takes only a second to become a child of God, but a whole lifetime to become the man or woman of God's design. Those who are given leadership charge over the church are to be people of proven maturity; spiritual long-distance runners, not over-enthusiastic sprinters. They must be graduates of the Christian life School of Hard Knocks, not just those with a diploma from a short-term discipleship course.

The original Greek word translated here as self-controlled is the word *sophron*. It meant literally "sober-minded". It described a person with a sane assessment of who he or she is before God and others, not puffed up or proud, but humble and fully cognisant of God's grace toward them. Have you ever noticed how those men and women that we really look up to and admire as godly, are almost always incredibly humble and self-effacing? We see them as spiritual giants, but they see themselves as mere sinners, saved by grace. That is the kind of spiritual maturity and sane self-perception of the elder.

Likewise, the person worthy of eldership is free from addiction to things like wealth and materialism and mind-altering substances (like alcohol); not intoxicated with greed for more "things". An elder is not a person who loses control of himself in drunkenness. Perhaps Paul had in mind the contrast he drew in Ephesians 5:18 between drunkenness with wine and being filled with the Holy Spirit:

> *Do not get drunk with wine, which leads to debauchery. Instead be filled with the Spirit . . .*

The qualification for eldership is being filled with the Holy

Spirit and having a walk with the Lord that is disciplined and dedicated. Time spent in the counsel of God's word and on their knees before God produces a Christian whose life is under God's control. Because of that relationship, they are able to encourage and help others.

That kind of spiritual maturity doesn't happen overnight. That's not to say that a relatively young person cannot be appointed to the office of elder. As mentioned in above, Timothy was noted for his youthfulness, and he was an elder in his church. Yet despite his youth there was also the mark of maturity and a relationship with the Lord that earned the respect and followership of others.

3. The Interpersonal Relationship Skills of an Elder

Those appointed to eldership are to be people who have learned to control themselves in their relations with others. There are seven qualities that Paul mentions to Timothy and Titus: *Temperate, not overbearing, not quick tempered, not violent, not quarrelsome, gentle, and able to teach.*

One word comes to mind that sums up at least six of these seven qualities: approachable. The person qualified for eldership is someone you can approach without fear of being abused. Someone who can listen to a different opinion without flying off the handle. Someone who can receive a different point of view without losing his cool.

Perhaps the word temperate best sums it up. Temperament or reactions are under control. A temperate person is not known for his or her "short wick;" they are not easily angered. They know the difference between responding and reacting. The person who is intemperate is a hot-head, whereas the temperate person thinks twice before responding. The overbearing person always wants to get his or her own way, is egotistical, arrogant and entrenched in their convictions. When an opinion is stated metaphorical concrete is poured around it - making it hard for them to budge! In contrast, the person who is not overbearing allows room for the convictions of others. He or she doesn't trust their own judgment to the extent that they will not hear how others view an issue.

The man or woman of God is not quarrelsome and contentious. They are not a fault-finder or a nitpicker or uncooperative to new ideas. Instead of dealing harshly with people, they recognise God is still at work in them and others. They have forbearance with the shortcomings of other brothers and sisters in Christ, because they know that they themselves are still in need of God's grace.

When Paul talked about the quality of being able to teach there are two possible ways it can be understood. The first is perhaps the most obvious: an ability to be able to communicate spiritual truths to others. Perhaps even a special "gifting" in that regard. 1 Timothy 5:17 certainly speaks of some elders having that ability to be able to train up others in the ways of God. But the original Greek text could also be translated as teach-able. In other words, a person who is able to be taught; willing to receive instruction and advice from others. The quality of being teachable is the attribute of humility. Someone willing to learn new truth, from whomever God would use to bring it, is the kind of person fit to be appointed as an elder.

4. The Family Life of an Elder

There are three remaining qualities that Paul mentions: *Husband of one wife, someone who manages his own family well, and hospitality.*

An elder is the husband of one wife. In our culture that's easy. It is against the law to have more than one spouse anyway. It wasn't in Paul's day. However, the intent of his instruction is still applicable. An elder is a person of sexual purity. He is a one-woman-man (or a one-man-woman), who has eyes and a heart for only his/her spouse: a person who is not flirtatious toward people of the opposite sex, who honours and cherishes his/her spouse, rather than putting them down or offending them. Those qualified for eldership treat their marriage with the utmost respect and priority. Dishonouring one's spouse is a disqualification from spiritual leadership.

Likewise, his or her attitude toward the rest of their family must be above reproach. How can a person have charge over the affairs of the church if their own family is in tatters or chaos? The story is told of a man who visited a church in another town. The preacher delivered an absolutely brilliant sermon, and the man was very impressed. He commented to people afterwards how good the preacher was and how lucky they must feel to have him as their pastor. However, the people shrugged their shoulders, and all looked glum and bored. Finally, one person said to the visitor, "Yeah, it's true, he does preach a good sermon. But you should see the way he treats his wife and kids!"

The measure of a truly godly leader is the way in which they relate with their family. Our work for God begins at home. If a person lacks the respect of their own family, can they command the respect of the church? Obviously, that is not to say that the children of an elder are going to be perfect or will always grow up to be Christians. Managing our families well will not automatically mean that our children will be or behave as model Christians. No matter how good a job we do of parenting, our children must choose for themselves whether they will love and follow Jesus. God has no grandchildren, only children! But the mark of a godly person, fit for the office of elder, will be the manner in which God is honoured in his or her home. If the home is not under control, particularly with young children, how on earth can that person be expected to manage the affairs of God's church?

Finally, the quality of hospitality. There is a tremendous amount that could be said about this as it relates to the qualification of an elder. Hospitable people are those who share what they have with others, who open their home to brothers and sisters in Christ, even to strangers. They have the quality of being unselfish with possessions.

Hospitality was at the very heart of what it meant to be a Christian in the early church. Homes were constantly open to brothers and sisters in God's family. They spent a lot of time with each other, and shared meals and resources, not only with those who could repay them with the same compliment, but also (perhaps especially) with those who couldn't afford to.

Hospitality is at the heart of what it means to be Christian in our day and age also. It is a feature of normal Christianity. Sadly, in our day we have often tended to become sub-normal Christians. Hospitality in many cases has become a lost art in the life of a healthy church. We need to do something about that. And the people who ought to be leading us into a fresh discovery of the joy of hospitality are those we appoint to the office of elder. It is specifically listed by Paul as one of the prerequisites. An elder, and his or her family, leads in hospitality.

In summary, it needs to be stressed again that these qualifications for eldership are not a score card in the hands of the church against those who might aspire to the office of elder. They are qualities of godliness and spiritual maturity for us all. Until or unless we have perfected them in our lives we need to be cautious about judging and criticising their absence in the lives of others. The log in our own eye means we can't see too well in picking out the speck in the eyes of others. They are, however, a guide-line for recognising and determining those in our midst whom we would appoint to an essential office.

THREE

OUR RELATIONSHIP TOWARD ELDERS

As noted in Chapter One, according to Acts 14:23 whenever Paul and Barnabas planted a church in their missionary journeys they appointed elders. It was the responsibility of those elders to watch over their church's operation and development. They operated in a role of spiritual leadership and pastoral oversight. We've turned the spotlight onto some of the specific functions of elders that are mentioned in the Scriptures, and also the necessary qualifications for eldership, most of which have to do with character and maturity rather than spiritual "gifting".

In this Chapter we shift the spotlight off those called to eldership and shine it onto the congregation as a whole: those people in the church whom elders are called to lead. We need to consider the way we are called of God to relate towards those people charged with eldership responsibilities. The New Testament has some specific advice regarding the manner in which we view the office of an elder, and there are many lessons that the modern-day church needs to learn in this regard.

Consider, for instance, the following four passages that speak of our relationship towards those in eldership:

1 Timothy 5:17-20
The elders who direct the affairs of the church well are worthy of double honour, especially those whose work is preaching and teaching. For the Scripture says, "Do not muzzle the ox while it is treading out the grain," and "The worker deserves his wages." Do not entertain an accusation against an elder unless it is brought by two or three witnesses. Those who sin are to be rebuked publicly, so that the others may take warning.

1 Thessalonians 5:12,13
Now we ask you, brothers, to respect those who work hard among you, who are over you in the Lord and who admonish you.Hold them in the highest regard in love because of their work. Live in peace with each other.

Hebrews 13:7
Remember your leaders, who spoke the word of God to you. Consider the outcome of their way of life and imitate their faith.

Hebrews 13:17
Obey your leaders and submit to their authority. They keep watch over you as men who must give an account. Obey them so that their work will be a joy, not a burden, for that would be of no advantage to you.

From these passages four principles emerge concerning the relationship on the part of church members toward those appointed to the office of elder in the local church.

1. Eldership is a God-ordained office in the church that we are to respect

We need to acknowledge a healthy tension between two theological principles that appear paradoxical. On the one hand the New Testament teaches emphatically the doctrine of the "priesthood of all believers." All Christians are priests before God in the sense that they are able to enter into personal relationship and communication with Almighty God, and to be his representative before others. There is no need for an intermediary "priest" to tell us what God wants for us or from us; each of us is able to hear and discern the will of God for ourselves. We don't need intermediary leaders to tell us what to do.

On the other hand, the New Testament also emphatically teaches the appointment and position of leadership in the church. While God is the leader and proprietor of his church, it has always been God's practice to allow and sanction the appointment of leaders over his people. In every chapter in the life of the Christian church (and the Old Testament before that) God has chosen to raise up spiritual leaders to lead and guide his people into the fulfilment of their mission.

Both of these two apparently paradoxical positions are able to be taken to an illogical extreme and, like me, you can probably think of examples where it has happened. Taking the "priesthood of all believers" to an illogical extreme results in a kind of spiritual anarchy. In its extreme, we don't need the institution and interference of a church and its leadership. Instead, it is essentially just me and Jesus! There is a lot that could be said about that: suffice it to note that it is not a theological position consistent with what the Bible teaches. Likewise, many leaders in churches have taken their perceived authority too far and have tended to operate as dictators and autocrats. Because of their position of leadership, they have chosen not to listen to the advice and discernment of the other "priests" in the family of God.

Now, without launching into a debate over styles of church government, we need to recognise there is a healthy tension between these two theological positions. The point to clarify, however, is that the appointment of people to the office of leadership and eldership in the church is something that God has instituted, and therefore it is an office that we are to honour and respect.

By virtue of the fact that Paul stresses the need to honour the office of elder in two separate letters, to two different churches, it might be logical to assume that this was an issue the New Testament churches wrestled with also.

> *1 Timothy 5:17*
> *The elders who direct the affairs of the church are worthy of double honour . . .*

> *1 Thessalonians 5:12*
> *Now we ask you, brothers, to respect those who work hard among you, who are over you in the Lord and who admonish you . . .*

Turning that around the other way, to hold leaders in the church with disregard or contempt or cynicism is quite clearly in conflict with what the Bible teaches. It is a sin against the church, and something for which we will be judged. As mentioned, this is an aspect of discipleship that many in the present-day church need to come to terms with.

Tall Poppy Syndrome!

We need also to recognise just how much the contemporary Christian church has taken on board the ways of the world and the culture in which we live. It may well be true for other cultures also, but in the New Zealand context with which I am most familiar we have gained somewhat of a sociological reputation as "poppy-choppers". Look out anyone who stands up in the political crowd and seeks to lead. They immediately become the target of aggression and hostility. For instance, when was the last time you saw a media commentator congratulate politicians for something they've said or done? Instead the media always present itself as pitted against those in positions of leadership, and that attitude of aggression toward leaders has filtered down throughout the entire nation. That it is not a reputation we should be proud of. In fact, the way we treat those in positions of political leadership is often sinful, a reproach against our nation that potentially brings us under a curse.

In the context of the church, the question needs to be asked: Have we imbibed some of the ways of the world in respect to our attitude towards those in spiritual leadership? Paul quite specifically commands us to honour and respect the office of elder. It is a God-ordained position in the life of a local church, and one that is to be respected. Paul's original words had to do with attitude of the heart, with highly esteeming or appreciating the necessity of the office. We are to regard those in the position of eldership as fulfilling a function that God has set in place. To dishonour or discredit them is to dishonour or discredit something that God has done.

It doesn't mean that we are to bow and scrape and defer to those in eldership when they walk by. That is not at all what Paul is talking about here. Rather he is dealing with the attitude we hold toward those in leadership positions. Do we thank God for them? Do we pray for them? Do we encourage them in the fulfilment of their assignment, honouring their office and function as something God has set in place in his church?

2. God Views Criticism of Leaders Seriously

This is not a particularly pleasant subject to deal with, but it needs to be faced. Unfair criticism and defamation of anyone is regarded by God as sin. However, it seems apparent from the Scriptures that unfair criticism and maligning of spiritual leaders in the household of God is treated seriously. It is not a small matter.

Now, I lay stress here on the word "unfair" criticism. Obviously, being in a position of eldership does not ever make one above criticism per se. Everyone is to be open to rebuke and correction, from whomever the Lord might choose to use. The issue Paul was raising, however, is whether or not the criticism is able to be substantiated.

> *1 Timothy 5:19*
> *Do not entertain an accusation against an elder unless it is brought by two or three witnesses . . .*

Perhaps Paul was referring to the power of words spoken against someone, like the power of a rumour. Someone once likened the power of a rumour to that of a long-range weapon. In order to strike you physically I have to be right alongside you. With a rumour, however, or a false accusation, I can hurt you and defame you from the other side of the world.

In terms of spiritual warfare and strategy, it stands to reason that the enemy of the church is going to attack those in leadership as a priority. It is good strategy. Take out the leaders and you bring the whole church down. Who will want to associate with a church that has leaders who are rumoured to be . . .?

There is a lot of talk today about the abuse of power by spiritual leaders. Many people have been deeply wounded by church leaders who have been manipulative and controlling and have overstepped lines of pastoral authority. There are a number of books that have been written about this kind of abuse of spiritual power and authority. It is a very real concern. Ever increasing numbers of people have opted out of church life altogether because they have been hurt by church leaders.

But there are two sides to this coin. Without denying the existence of spiritual and leadership abuse, there is another side to the spiritual abuse issue. That has to do with the ever-increasing numbers of church leaders, and their wives and families, who have been abused and deeply wounded by the people in the churches they are called to lead. The pendulum of spiritual abuse in the church swings both ways.

I well remember the skepticism I felt in a Pastoral Care lecture at Theological College when the lecturer suggested we take a good look around at who was in our class. He then suggested that in five-to-ten years at least 60% of them would no longer be in pastoral ministry. The pressure and tension and stress would have got to them, and to save their marriages and families they would have left the pastoral ministry. I remember thinking, what a load of garbage! We're all in this for life. Looking back over the years, I can see that that lecturer was absolutely right!

Likewise, I remember the comments when I began my journey into pastoral ministry in the late '70s. When you told friends what you were doing for a job, oft-times you would hear comments like: *"Boy, what a neat job. Working full-time for the Lord, helping people grow spiritually. What a neat calling . . . etc."* Nowadays the comments you hear when you mention that you are a pastor can go something like, *"No way man . . . not me! You'd have to be crazy to want to be a pastor (or a pastor's wife!) . . . being the butt of all that criticism and stress and tension . . . etc."*

We need to own up to the fact that churches can at times be quite cruel toward those in spiritual leadership. A wise wife of a retired pastor friend once made the following comment, and it has been indelibly printed on my mind: *"Pastoral ministry is sometimes like being the anvil on which people beat out their faith!"*

Of course, that kind of stress and criticism toward spiritual leaders is not a new phenomenon. It is recorded as happening right throughout the Scriptures. However, the Scriptures also expound the attitude of God towards those who malign leaders, and grumble against them, and say things which are cruel and defamatory. David was a man of God who knew he was called to be king of Israel. He knew his calling before God, and the position of honour he would one day hold as king. Yet David refused to dishonour Saul, the current king. Even though Saul had become incredibly corrupt and spiritually bankrupt, David's response was:

1 Samuel 26:11
. . . the Lord forbid that I should lay a hand on the Lord's anointed

Judgement on the maligners

Numbers 16 is another telling example. Korah, Dathan and Abiram grumbled and murmured against Moses and Aaron. They spread false rumours amongst the Israelites about the character and integrity of their leaders. It went on for some time and was extremely painful for Moses. In the end the Lord acted. Those who were persistent in murmuring and spreading false accusations against their leaders in the Lord were simply removed from the community. In fact, so dramatically did he act that the ground opened up beneath them and swallowed them up. God treats unfair and unjust criticism (defamation) of spiritual leaders as a serious offence. We do well to be warned!

Coming back to what Paul wrote to Timothy, it is interesting to note that Paul didn't merely instruct us not to speak an accusation against an elder. That is one thing. But he also said that we are not to entertain such an accusation when someone else drops it in our ear. The original Greek word there is *paradechomai*, and it meant literally "to receive or admit with approval". It is the deliberate and ready acceptance of an accusation against a spiritual leader. Until or unless it can be substantiated by two or three witnesses, we are not to receive it. Allowing someone to make an unsubstantiated accusation, according to what Paul instructed Timothy, is tantamount to showing hospitality to their words.

The Scriptures are very clear on how conflict is to be resolved, and how a brother or sister who sins is to be confronted and rebuked. It is always, in the first instance, to be done person to person, never spoken about to others. That is gossip, and the Bible condemns gossip as sin. When we allow someone else to speak in a defamatory way against a brother or sister in Christ, we also become guilty of their sin. Better that we stop them and say: *"Please don't tell me . . . you should go and see that person directly."* Or perhaps even, *"Come on . . . let's go together and see that person and check out whether the accusation you have made is true."* More on this in the next Chapter.

3. Leadership in the Kingdom of God is by Example

Here is a challenge to those in positions of spiritual leadership. As the people of God, we are exhorted by the writer to the Hebrews to:

> *Hebrews 13:7*
> *Remember your leaders, who spoke the Word of God to you. Consider the outcome of their way of life and imitate their faith.*

In most countries today, the shepherd rounds up his sheep and directs them from the back, using dogs to chase and frighten them into submission. That is not the definition of the spiritual shepherd in the Bible. The Middle Eastern shepherd always walked in front of his flock. The sheep knew the sound of the shepherd's voice, and they followed him, even when they passed alongside another flock and its shepherd.

Leading the flock of God is always done from the front, showing the way; not from behind, barking out orders. To be a leader in the family of God is to be a role model, an example of what others are expected to be or do.

The story is told of generals during World War I who reputedly sat behind the safety of their own lines, issuing orders to their troops to keep advancing against the enemy. While they sat and pontificated in relative security they were oblivious to the fact that the enemy had their front-line troops completely surrounded. The orders they passed down the line were like an execution warrant to their troops.

In spiritual warfare the elders don't sit behind closed doors in the war office; they fight in the trenches. They don't merely encourage and exhort the church to go out into the world and battle the enemy, they go out themselves into the front lines, and lead the people into whatever the Lord is calling the church into. That's why Paul sounds the strong and public rebuke for the elder caught in sin:

> *1 Timothy 5:20*
> *Those who sin are to be rebuked publicly, so that others may take warning . . .*

Eldership means role modelling - being an example in faith and righteousness and spiritual maturity. In the same way that a policeman caught breaking the law is treated very harshly by the courts, so too the elder who sets a bad example. That's why Jesus sharply criticised the Pharisees and teachers of the law in his day. They taught and expected others to obey the law, but they themselves didn't keep it. If God treats unjustified criticism of spiritual leaders as a serious issue, likewise those in eldership need to be aware of God's attitude toward those who set a bad example.

4. Leaders Must Be Allowed to Lead

Hebrews 13:17 is for me a hugely instructive text for when it comes to leaders leading, and followers following. Sadly, it has often been misunderstood and misused. The NIV translation (1973,1978, 1984) renders it this way:[5]

> *Obey your leaders and submit to their authority. They keep watch over you as men who must give an account. Obey them so that their work will be a joy, not a burden, for that would be of no advantage to you.*

Read this verse in many churches today and you can observe the people move forward in their seats a centimetre or two! Texts like this one have been used to great advantage (or more correctly, disadvantage) by autocratic church leaders who have wanted to whip their congregations into submission. It has not infrequently been played like a "trump card" by an insecure pastor and/or eldership who aren't getting their own way. Another verse that is sometimes touted alongside it is Samuel's rebuke to king Saul in 1 Samuel 15:23: "*Rebellion is as the sin of witchcraft . . .!*" The leadership pull rank on the people, and they submit for fear of divine wrath.[6]

---

5 Similarly, most other English translations. For example:
Obey your leaders and submit to them . . . (RSV)
Obey your leaders and submit to them . . . (NASB)
Obey them that have the rule over you, and submit yourselves . . . (KJV)
Obey your leaders and do what they say . . . (CEV)

6 While serving as National Leader for the Baptist Churches of NZ I was once asked to consult with a church where the elders were proposing a highly controversial project, for which there was resistance from some church members. The elders had pulled Hebrews 13:17 out and told the people they were to obey what was being proposed because of their office!

The shepherd is my lord

I suspect the writer to the Hebrews would cringe to think his (or her) words were being misused in this fashion. In fact, I feel so strongly about that as to suggest that whenever a church leader pulls rank on his or her congregation they have lost all credibility as a leader. That was not at all the intention of this verse. A few decades ago there were some disturbing trends in respect to authoritarian leadership styles in the church. Instead of the people of God standing in their God-given positions as priests, they were instructed not to make any major decisions in life without first checking it with the counsel of their shepherd. Now, seeking the wisdom and counsel of others is, of course, a healthy practice, and we wouldn't want to discourage that. However, in some circles it devolved to an unhealthy extreme, perhaps even the inversion of the first line of the 23rd Psalm: *the shepherd is now my lord!*

How then are to understand and appropriate what the writer of Hebrews 13:17 is calling for? At face value some might think it calls for blind obedience to leaders, merely because they are of a higher rank or station; those who are not leaders are thereby subordinate and expected to just comply. Or is there perhaps a subtle nuance here that calls for obedience on the basis of perceived trust and agreement with the one who is leading?

My understanding of the particular word translated as "obey" in this verse is that it is not so much based upon hierarchy and rank on the part of the leader, as upon winsome persuasion of those he or she leads. The word, *peitho*, has the inference of persuasive process about a proposed change or action that followers of leaders are asked to take. Obedience is called for, yes, but on the basis of having been persuaded. In other words, healthy leadership allows for new ideas or proposals to settle or process or become used to. Obedience follows from having been persuaded that a particular course of action is to be followed.

Similarly, my understanding of the word translated as "submit" in this verse (*hupeiko*) includes the connotation of yielding or giving way; allowing leaders to lead. Perhaps the same idea as the "give way" or "yield" sign at the road intersection. Or imagine two people seeking to pass through a narrow doorway that is not wide enough for both to pass side-by-side; one yields way or submits to the other and allows them to go in front. Rather than barging on in one's own ideas and opinions, without giving anyone else a thought, followers of healthy leadership give way to allow them to go in front, falling in behind.

Obedience and submission in this context is far from militaristic or authoritarian; more a willing deferment to the character and authority of a leader who has won them over – perhaps by respecting them enough to give time and space to process why an action ought to be taken.

Surely this concept of leadership, and of followership, is consistent with how Jesus spoke of leadership within God's kingdom. He posited it as contradistinctive to the rulers of the Gentiles (Matthew 20:25; Mark 10:42; Luke 22:25) who demanded compliance with orders and instructions. By contrast, leaders in the way of Jesus serve and respect those they lead, and persuade them to their course, and part of that persuasion implies time and dialogue and the courtesy of giving good reason for change.

While we do not know for certain who the writer to the Hebrews was, it would seem reasonable to assume there was synergy with how the Apostles Peter and Paul approached the task of leadership. Peter specifically exhorted elders to not "lord" it over those under their care (1 Peter 5:3), and Paul references to the Corinthians that he did not "lord" it over their faith. Hebrews 13:17 is not to be used as an authoritarian premise – which it clearly has been in some circles. Words like "obey," "submit" and "authority" are clearly in this text for a reason, but behind them is a reciprocal courtesy.

Leaders are not to expect people in the church to support or comply with their instructions simply because they are the leaders. And church members are not subordinate underlings of those in leadership, and therefore have to do whatever they are told. There are many warnings in the Scriptures about testing what is said by prophets and teachers. The spiritual leader who will not (or cannot) explain and persuade people to follow a course of action, believed to be of the Lord, is simply not worthy of being followed. Giving cogent reasons for change of direction, and also time for people to process a new idea and to come on board, is part and parcel of the leadership mandate. On the other hand, however, we are also to adopt an attitude of heart that allows those in leadership to actually lead us.

I remember a friend some years ago telling me of an old Scottish friend of his who emigrated to New Zealand. One of the first comments he made when he got off the boat in Auckland was: "*Is there a government here? Well I'm agin it!*" Sadly, there are some people who approach leadership in the church with the same kind of twisted cynicism. They start from the position that all leaders in the church are power-hungry, manipulative maniacs, until proven otherwise. That is not a godly response or attitude toward leadership. Some of us in the family of God may need to break up the concrete that has set around our entrenched opinions and convictions. Leading people in the church of Jesus Christ is sometimes not dissimilar to moving a stubborn old mule. Not only does the Bible teach leadership; it also teaches followership, and some of us need to relearn how to be a follower of those who are called to lead.

If God in his wisdom has raised up people to lead his people, it is because he wants his people to be led. And that means that we allow those charged with leadership responsibility the room to move in front of us and lead. We need to give them opportunity to persuade us to follow the direction in which they are leading and giving way to them so that they can go in front and actually lead.

Maybe there is tremendous need in the contemporary church for emotional healing for those who have been wounded and abused by bad leaders. As noted, sadly, many abuses have taken place, and innocent people have been emotionally and spiritually crushed. A by-product of that has been an unwillingness to trust any other leadership in the future. Some who have been scarred by leaders in one situation, have wrongly assumed that every other church leader they come across will abuse them in the same way. That is simply not fair or justified. If we need healing because we've been hurt in the past, we need to seek ministry and healing. Our actions and attitudes in the present are never justified because of our past experience, no matter how bad it has been. That would be like saying the man who sexually abuses a child is somehow justified and exonerated because he himself was a victim of abuse as a child. He is not. Two wrongs never make a right! There is not a lot we can do about our past experiences except to forgive those who have hurt us, and to put down our bitterness.

What we do however have power over is that which we do with the future. If God has given us leaders in the church it is because he thinks we need them. It is not an office that many find easy, and to be sure those called to the office of elder are singled out by the evil one for special assault. Because leaders are human they will sometimes act with imperfection – that shouldn't surprise us. However, we can be equally sure that God will answer all the prayers we offer up to him for wisdom and grace and anointing upon those appointed as our elders.

Why not pause right now and thank God for your elders and pray a blessing upon them!

FOUR

ELDERS ARE NOT OMBUDSMEN!

This closing Chapter is really a postscript and focuses on one aspect of eldership that I have observed go horribly wrong in many churches. In addition to pastoring local churches I have also served in national denominational leadership roles in two countries and consulted with a numerous of churches in the work of conflict resolution. What I raise here is born of observation (and some personal experience) that we might be able to learn from.

Interpersonal relationships in the church can be interesting and tricky at times. We strive for unity and harmony, for we know that is where the Lord commands his blessing (Psalm 133), but sometimes it doesn't work out that way. From time to time, in every church, there will be people who feel offended, aggrieved or miffed in some way, or they will observe things that they believe ought to be addressed. To whom do they turn in such situations and how are these types of issues best processed?

While the New Testament records a number of statements about processes for conflict resolution, and the importance of confronting inappropriate behavior, in the minds of many

Christians today the people in a local church to whom they turn for resolution are often those appointed as elders. Elders are perceived as the ones responsible for dealing with shortcomings in the life of a church, and perhaps especially when the pastoral staff are viewed as the cause. In cases of serious misconduct, the elders are obviously the ones who carry such responsibility. However, in many instances issues of conflict or disagreement are relatively minor and when these are referred to, and engaged with, by elders, can lead to confused lines of accountability – resulting in breaches of trust.

Over the forty years I have served as a pastor I have seen a recurring scenario play out that causes tension amongst elderships, and especially between a group of elders and the (senior) pastor. Relationships become strained and the door for disunity cracks open, which invariably has a deleterious effect upon the church as a whole. It occurs when members of an eldership assume, perhaps unintentionally, the function of *ombudsman*.

By definition, an ombudsman is someone charged with hearing, investigating and attempting to resolve complaints. They are theoretically impartial and are supposed to be objective. They can be as official as a government office, and they also operate in certain industries (such as insurance or banking) as a place for appeal when consumers believe they are receiving a raw deal. In principle, the office of ombudsman is a great idea, especially as a foil against corrupt and bullying institutions. Indeed, some may even think it is a valuable role to establish in a local church, especially one where leadership is perceived to be strong.

It is not, I would contend, the function of those who assume the role of eldership!

There can be a pernicious and volatile change in culture

amongst a leadership team that takes them by surprise. It often occurs when new people are invited to join a leadership team, or with new appointments of associate pastoral staff - especially when appointed from within the church. It can be especially painful when close friends of a pastor are recruited by him/her to a role of leadership. Within a matter of months an observable change in their loyalty and friendship begins to surface that is puzzling and is often caused by the new leader beginning to hear grumbling and grizzles that they didn't know about before their appointment. Indeed, there is well warn caution for pastors employing close friends for this reason.

There are several predictable reasons why this malaise can occur. In the minds of many ordinary church members, newly appointed elders (and/or associate pastoral staff) are viewed as fair game for those wanting to express a complaint, either in general or perhaps with the pastor in particular. Complainants may feel they have not been adequately heard in the past, or their viewpoint ignored by those in leadership. With someone new coming onto the team there is a natural, perhaps understandable, opportunity for new "ears" to hear and potentially re-litigate their grievance. New appointees to leadership, who may have accepted nomination with a view to making a difference, can become unintentional "honey pots" around which "grizzly bees" are attracted. Without clear understanding of boundaries and the potential for this kind of scenario, more than a few new appointees have found themselves forming a jaundiced view of their pastor, whom they once respected and maybe thought "walked on water." Without perhaps appreciating all the issues traversed beforehand, they become deeply disappointed at his/her "clay feet" and in some instances seek to become the champions of reform and correction.

Marshall Shelley, in his excellent book: *"Well-Intentioned Dragons"* (Bethany House Publishers, 1994) warns new pastors to be cautious of those who overly ingratiate themselves to them upon commencement of their ministry. He cautions that some may have a mischievous agenda hoping they can recruit a new pastor to their way of thinking by presenting themselves as "new best friends," only to withdraw and turn on the new pastor a few months later when he or she doesn't appear to be seeing things their way. I have experienced this over the years, and the same scenario can occur with new appointees to the office of eldership, or to associate staff positions.

The function of eldership is NOT an office of ombudsman in a local church. There are several reasons why I believe this is important to clarify.

Firstly, starting with Scripture, we noted in Chapter Four Paul's clear instruction to Timothy:

1 Timothy 5:19
. . . do not entertain an accusation against an elder unless it is brought by two or three witnesses.

The first thing to note from this is that accusations against an elder or pastor must be serious and empirically verifiable before they are to be taken seriously. Apparently, the idea of critiquing leaders in the church is not something new to our era. There were frivolous and vexatious niggles amongst the Ephesian church leaders in Timothy's day also, and such complaints were not to be entertained unless serious and attested.

To be sure, the very next verse warns that if there is substantive sin (one assumes this might be something continual and un-repented over, not just a minor mistake) then appropriate reproof is necessary before the church. However, the issue that can sometimes trip up an unsuspecting elder is the "entertaining" of illegitimate accusations. The very act of listening to and receiving a complaint can imply validation of its substance (to both the complainant and the elder), and the further investigation of such accusations certainly means the accusation has been entertained and found a home.

Secondly, the nature of pastoral leadership invariably confronts inappropriate behavior in the church. Indeed, so much of the New Testament had occasion to be recorded because there was much poor behavior that conflicted with God's ideal. Therefore, it should never be a surprise that at times there will be people with a miff or a grizzle. Sometimes the nature of pastoral ministry requires confrontation. Sometimes a good shepherd needs to stand in the way of a wolf. Often times good leadership requires the overcoming of congregational inertia, and in the process, those sitting in resistant comfort become annoyed at the idea of change. In fact, it could even be contended that without change in the church, and all the discomfort that it brings, there is a discernable absence of leadership - the status quo doesn't require anything to happen!

Early in my Christian leadership experience I came across a little saying that has shaped my thinking around change management: *"Change means movement, and movement means friction, and friction means heat, and heat means conflict. You just can't get a rocket off the ground discreetly and quietly."*

In other words, the presence per se of conflict or grizzles amidst the life of a church can be perfectly normal and predictable. That is not to suggest license for rudeness or treating people inappropriately, but it does imply a lack of surprise when some don't like or appreciate a good leader who is moving people out of their comfort zone. It might even be testament that a pastor is doing the right things, as Paul suggested to Timothy in his second letter:

> *2 Timothy 4:2*
> *. . . correct, rebuke and encourage – with great patience and careful instruction.*

Effective pastoral leadership is more than merely *encouragement* and tender care; there is also the uncomfortable injunction here to *correct* and *rebuke* as well, and that is not always welcome or appreciated.

The notion that when everything is done in a local church just the way God wants it, there will be perfect harmony and the absence of any conflict, is simply naïve and not at all consistent with New Testament experience. Even Jesus had his detractors . . . and look what they eventually did to him!

Thirdly, elders are actually not neutral. And neutrality is a critical component of an ombudsman's function. To be an elder is NOT to stand aloof or independent from the pastoral staff, especially the church's pastor. The relationship is inherently close and inextricably connected. An individual elder, or a group of elders as a whole, does not stand on the sidelines of interpersonal relationships in the church, seeking to give independent advice. Elders are in the middle of the play and operate together as a tight team. In fact, for an elder(s) to accept the role of ombudsman is a bit like being in a member of our favourite sports team and playing a simultaneous role as referee. It is foul play!

In some churches there is also a practice (formal or informal) of elders representing different sections or lobby groups in the life of the congregation. Sometimes this is reinforced by distribution of representative portfolios. There is need for caution in this. Taking John Carver's *"Policy Governance Model"* as a template, members of an Elder Board actually represent the vision of the church as a whole, not segments or ministry groups within that vision. In fact, Carver goes further and suggests that a Board primarily represents the owner(s) of the enterprise and is committed to ensuring that the owner's purposes, vision and aspirations are fulfilled - even at the cost of conflict with some of those they lead.[7]

This of course begs the question: Who are the owners of the church? There are different answers (and nuances to those answers) to this kind of question. Some may perceive church ownership is represented by the members of the church, who appoint or elect the elders, as they are the stakeholders and therefore congisance of what they say must be duly taken. If they raise a concern it needs to be considered seriously. Others argue that ownership of the church rests unilaterally with God, not the members of the church. The church is the body of Christ, not the body of its constituent members. God owns the church, and that is whom elders are ultimately accountable to, despite varied political machinations by which they are appointed.

I am certainly not suggesting that appointed leaders are unimpeachable and therefore not able to be questioned or disagreed with. Heaven forbid! Regardless of agreed polity and processes for decision-making, members of a church must always feel free to discuss issues and ideas and even hold to a different opinion. The issue under discussion here is more about those grizzles and

---

[7] For a fuller summary of John Carver's *"Policy Governance Model"* see my book *"A New Kind of Baptist Church – Reframing Congregational Government for the 21st Century,"* (Morling Press, 2010) – Chapter 10.

niggles when decisions have been made that some find contentious, resulting in criticism of a senior leader(s).

The point is, an elder who hears or receives a complaint is not a neutral independent party. Elders work through issues together and are honour-bound by the commitment to uphold caucus-made decisions. They are part of the tight team of leaders who represent the owner's ambition, and if Carver's model has any sway, they are collegial members with the pastor. They have a bias in loyalty, commitment and respect.

That doesn't inherently mean they cannot disagree with other members of their tight team. By all means, enjoy robust debate and differing convictions within the context of a meeting. But it is critical that elders do not project to church members autonomy and independence from the pastor and the rest of the elder team.

Fourthly, the position of eldership does not abrogate the advice Jesus gives concerning appropriate conflict resolution. Matthew 18:15-17 is generally regarded as the best model for dispute resolution.

> *If your brother or sister sins, go and point out their fault, just between the two of you. If they listen to you, you have won them over. But if they will not listen, take one or two others along, so that 'every matter may be established by the testimony of two or three witnesses.' If they still refuse to listen, tell it to the church; and if they refuse to listen even to the church, treat them as you would a pagan or a tax collector.*

While it may not always equate with the types of issues elders are approached about, the principles apply. The person who is aggrieved is first to approach the person they believe is responsible, and to seek to sort things out one-on-one. They do not go to a third party and confess someone else's sin or misdemeanor. First course of action is to/with the person concerned. Only after that recourse has not altered or resolved an issue is the matter taken further to a second party, and if still unresolved to the church.

Where does this apply to the church member approaching an elder over a grievance with, say, the pastor? It implies that the elder receiving such commentary should stop the supposed aggrieved party in their tracks, asking instead if they have been to the person concerned and talked it through with them. If they have not, the elder should stop the conversation and insist that this ought to be the course taken.

Of course, one of the easy excuses for an aggrieved person not following the process Jesus advised is that they do not believe they can "safely" approach a church leader. Maybe this is sometimes the case, but in my experience the veracity of such an assertion is rare. It is simply an easy claim to make but may not in fact be valid or true. If there is any sense of validity to apparent imbalance of power (e.g. a church member approaching a pastor over an alleged grievance) it might be the place of an elder to broker a meeting. In other words, offering to go with a person to meet with the leader, or potentially setting something up whereby a meeting can occur. But this is a very different role to one of ombudsman, who seeks to investigate and potentially mediate a solution.

Fifthly, the toleration of gossip and slander in the life of a local church is extremely destructive. It plays into the hands of the evil one who wants nothing more than to see disunity and factionalism take root. And that is the nature of most grievances taken by church members to an elder! Gossip and slander were among the things Paul feared he would find when visiting the Corinthian church (2 Corinthians 12:20), and it is not something to be left unchecked. Elders who listen to and accommodate gossip and slander, without allowing the target of such commentary the dignity of fair response before forming of an opinion, can be guilty of driving a wedge of disunity into the life of a church.

By all means there may be a case for establishing an appropriate disputes resolution process in the life of a local church. The concept behind an ombudsman is not inappropriate per se. Indeed, most employment contracts include a process by which disputes can be handled constructively. But such procedures call for wisdom and caution. Maybe it could be a role played by former elders or a retired pastor in the church – who understands the dynamics of leadership and what it is like *"herding cats."*

However, in my view it is not automatically the purview of those called to the office of eldership, as their role is inextricably and symbiotically linked with senior leadership. While elders are typically the ones to whom a pastor is primarily accountable, the weighting on the role of elders ought to be one of love and support and resourcing for achievement. They are not the "opposition party" to the leader or pastor, with the role of critiquing and "keeping them honest!"

www.ingramcontent.com/pod-product-compliance
Ingram Content Group UK Ltd.
Pitfield, Milton Keynes, MK11 3LW, UK
UKHW020418250726
13967UKWH00007B/2704

9 780473 436681